MASTERING STOCK
OPTIONS

The secrets they don't want you to know

BRANDON ARTHUR

TABLE OF CONTENTS

CHAPTER 1: Introduction to Stocks 3

What is a Stock.. 3

What are Stock options 3

Understanding Option Contracts... 4

Why trade stock options 5

Basic Option Terminology... 6

CHAPTER 2: The Mechanism of Stock Options 9

What is a Candlestick?..10

Why are candlesticks important?...10

Bullish Candle Stock goes up:..11

Bearish Candle- Stock goes down:..11

How to read candlesticks and candlestick patterns 13

Option Pricing & Valuation 14

Intrinsic Value vs Time Value 15

Option premiums and factors affecting prices 16

Option expiration and exercise 18

CHAPTER 3: Option Strategies for Beginners 20

Long Calls and Puts 20

Covered Calls 21

Cash Secured Puts 23

Protective Puts 24

Bullish and Bearish Spreads...25

CHAPTER 4: Advanced Option Trading Strategies....................27

Iron Condors..27

Butterfly Spreads...28

Calendar Spread 29

Straddles and Strangles..30

Diagonal Spreads 32

CHAPTER 5: Risk Management and Position Sizing.............................. 34

Importance of Risk management...34

Determining Risk Tolerance 35

Stop Losses 37

Setting Stop losses...38

Position Sizing Strategies 40

CHAPTER 6: Fundamental and Technical Analysis for Options Trading................ 42

Evaluating Stocks for Options Trading..43

Analyzing Market trends and indicators..44

Using volatility to your advantage 46

Implementing Options Strategies based on Analysis 47

CHAPTER 7: Practical Tips for Successful Option Trading 50

Managing Emotions and Discipline..52

Learning from Mistakes and Adapting Strategies...............................54

Resources for Ongoing Education and Research 56

CHAPTER 8: Case Studies and Examples.. 59

Trade Examples for Different Strategies...59

Trend Following Strategy: 59

Mean Reversion Strategy: 59

Breakout & Retest Strategy:..60

Scalping Strategy: 62

Trade Simulations and Back testing Tools 62

Paper Trading 64

Here's how paper trading works:..64

CHAPTER 9: Conclusion 67

Unlock the Secrets of Stock Options: An In-Depth Guide

This comprehensive eBook offers a comprehensive guide to the world of stock options. It takes you through the basics and gradually introduces more advanced concepts and strategies. Packed with practical tips, case studies, and examples, this resource will equip you with the knowledge and skills needed for effective options trading. Whether you're starting out or an experienced trader. "Mastering Stock Options" will be your invaluable companion in navigating the complexities of the options market and achieving trading success. Wishing you happy trading.

DISCLAIMER

I am not a license broker, nor do I have a degree in finance or statistics. All my information in this eBook comes from research, courses, books, and personal experience. I, Brandon Arthur, use these strategies to give myself a swing and day trading advantage. I am not responsible for any risk you take trading short- or long-term investment using any of my strategies. I highly recommend non-experienced traders to NOT participate in option trading until they have educated themselves. Furthermore, I encourage beginners to start with paper trading first before jumping in the market. I do NOT give any business or anyone permission to sell my e-book or distribute it.

As a beginner it is important to take baby steps. Never Just dive into a stock trade because it's popular or because it was recommended by a friend without any supporting evidence. Most beginners' biggest fear is losing money in the stock market. All investors have lost some sort of money when trading on the market. Furthermore, focus on getting familiar with the stock market, books, courses, YouTube videos, and mentorships from experienced investors.

Usually new traders are in a hurry to try and get rich overnight by following other investors. When you first start off, know that you will not see huge gains overnight. In my opinion, it takes about a month or two for a portfolio to balance out. Since the "*Robin Hood*" app is extremely popular and user friendly I recommend starting off with that as a beginner. Working on being patient, risk management & having a willingness to learn is key to winning in the stock market.

My brother always taught me, "You can give a person a fish, but if you learn how to fish yourself, you'll never be hungry again!"

CHAPTER 1
Introduction to Stocks

What is a Stock

Stocks are the capital raised by a business or corporation through the subscription of shares. Shares are pieces of the company. Owning shares would make you a shareholder.

What are Stock options

Stock options are financial derivatives that give the holder the right, but not the obligation, to buy or sell a specific amount of underlying stock at a predetermined price (known as the strike price) within a specified time frame. They are contracts between two parties: the buyer, also known as the option holder, and the seller, referred to as the option writer.

There are two types of stock options: call options and put options. A call option gives the holder the right to buy the underlying stock, while a put option grants the holder the right to sell the underlying stock. These options provide investors with the opportunity to profit from price movements in the underlying stock without owning the stock itself.

Stock options are typically traded on exchanges and have standardized terms, including the expiration date (the last day the option can be exercised) and the strike price. The value of an option is influenced by factors such as the current stock price, the strike price, time remaining until expiration, market volatility, and interest rates.

Traders and investors use stock options for various purposes, including speculation, hedging against potential price movements, income generation through option selling, and strategic investment strategies. However, it's important to note that trading options involves risks and requires a solid understanding of the underlying stocks and options market dynamics.

1 Contract is = to 100 Shares.

Understanding Option Contracts

Option contracts are financial derivatives that give the holder the right, but not the obligation, to buy (call option) or sell (put option) an underlying asset at a predetermined price (strike price) within a specific period (expiration date). They are commonly used in financial markets for speculation, hedging, and risk management.

Call Options: Buying a call option grants the holder the right to purchase the underlying asset at the strike price before the expiration date. This is beneficial if the asset's price rises above the strike price, allowing the holder to buy at a lower price and potentially profit from the price difference.

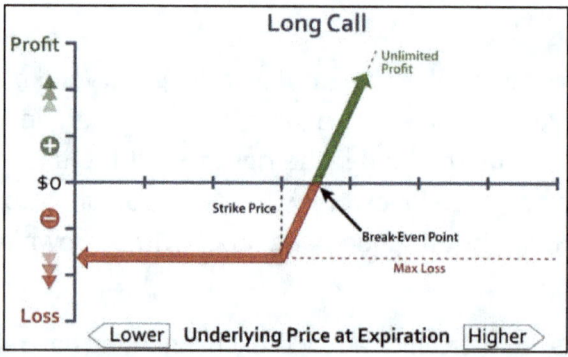

Put Options: Buying a put option gives the holder the right to sell the underlying asset at the strike price before the expiration date. This is advantageous if the asset's price falls below the strike price, enabling the holder to sell at a higher price and potentially profit from the price difference.

It's important to note that option contracts have an expiration date, and if the price of the underlying asset doesn't move favorably, the holder may choose not to exercise the option. In such cases, the option expires worthless, and the holder loses the premium paid to purchase the contract

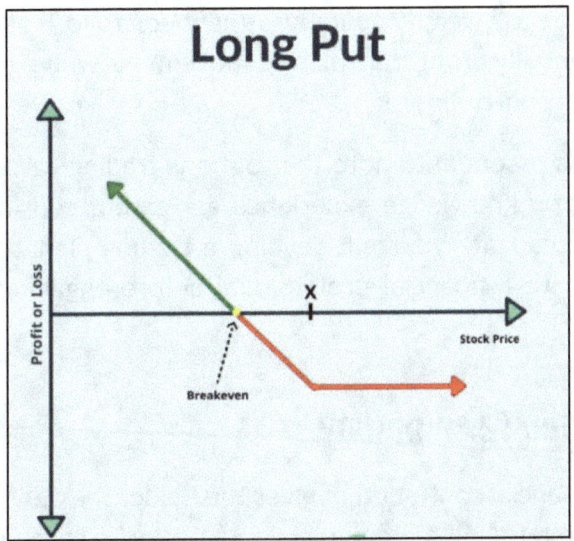

Why trade stock options

Trading stock options can offer several potential benefits:

1. **Leverage:** Options allow you to control a larger number of shares with a smaller investment compared to buying the underlying stock outright. This leverage can amplify your returns if the trade moves in your favor. 📱

2. **Flexibility:** Options provide various strategies to adapt to different market conditions. Whether you're bullish, bearish, or neutral, options allow you to implement strategies such as buying calls or puts, selling covered calls, or engaging in complex option spreads. 📱

3. Hedging: Options can act as a form of insurance to protect your stock portfolio against potential downside risks. By purchasing put options, you can limit your losses if the stock price declines.

4. Income generation: Selling options can generate premium income. By utilizing strategies like covered calls, you can earn additional income from your existing stock holdings. ▨

5. Diversification: Options trading can offer an additional avenue to diversify your investment portfolio. It allows you to potentially profit from market movements while reducing overall portfolio risk.

However, it's essential to note that options trading carries inherent risks. It requires knowledge, experience, and careful consideration. It's advisable to educate yourself, develop a trading plan, and consider consulting with a financial professional before engaging in options trading.

Basic Option Terminology

Option: A financial contract that gives the holder the right, but not the obligation, to buy (call option) or sell (put option) a specific asset (e.g., stock, commodity) at a predetermined price within a specified period.

Call Option: An option that gives the holder the right to buy the underlying asset at the predetermined price (strike price) before or on the expiration date.

Put Option: An option that gives the holder the right to sell the underlying asset at the strike price before or on the expiration date.

Strike Price: The predetermined price at which the underlying asset can be bought (in the case of a call option) or sold (in the case of a put option).

Expiration Date: The date on which the option contract expires and becomes void. After this date, the option can no longer be exercised.

Premium: The price paid by the option buyer to the option seller for acquiring the rights associated with the option contract.

In the Money (ITM): When the option's strike price is favorable compared to the current market price of the underlying asset. For calls, it means the market price is above the strike price; for puts, it means the market price is below the strike price.

Out of the Money (OTM): When the option's strike price is not favorable compared to the current market price of the underlying asset. For calls, it means the market price is below the strike price; for puts, it means the market price is above the strike price.

At the Money (ATM): When the option's strike price is approximately equal to the current market price of the underlying asset.

Portfolio - A collection of stocks bought by someone makes up their portfolio.

Bear Market- A bear market is a general decrease in the stock market within a timeframe. It includes a transition from high investor optimism to widespread investor fear and pessimism. Once generally accepted measure of a bear market is a price decline of 20% or more within a 2-month period.

Bull Market- A bull market is the condition of a financial market in which prices are increasing or are expected to rise.

Blue Chip- A blue chip stock is a huge company with an exceptional reputation. These are typically large, well-established, and popular companies that have operated for many years and that have steady earnings, often paying dividends to investors. Blue Chip stocks are usually good for long-term investments.

For Example: *Apple, Amazon, JP Morgan Chase, Walmart, Meta & Tesla*

Earnings per share: Earnings per share (EPS) is calculated as a company's profit divided by the outstanding shares of its common stock. The resulting number serves as an indicator of a company's profitability. The higher a company's EPS, the more profitable it is.

$$EPS = \frac{\text{Net Income - Preferred Dividends}}{\text{Weighted Average Shares Outstanding}}$$

Dividends- A stock dividend is a dividend payment to shareholders (You) that is made in shares rather than as cash. ... For example, a company might issue a stock dividend of 5%, which will require it to issue 0.05 shares for every share owned by existing shareholders, so the owner of 100 shares would receive five additional shares.

Bid- The term "bid" refers to the highest price a buyer will pay to buy a specified number of shares of a stock at any given time.

Ask- The term "ask" refers to the lowest price at which a seller will sell the stock.

Spread- Normally, the spread refers to the difference between two prices, rates, or yields. The spread is the gap between the bid and the asking prices of a stock or Bond.

Close- The close refers to the end of a trading session in the financial markets when the markets close for the day.

Volume - The number of shares of stock traded during a particular time, normally measured in average daily trading volume.

Yield - Often refers to the measure of the return on an investment that is received from the payment of a dividend.

CHAPTER 2
The Mechanism of Stock Options

Stock options are financial instruments that give individuals the right, but not the obligation, to buy or sell a specific number of shares in a company's stock at a predetermined price, known as the strike price, within a specified period. The mechanisms of stock options involve several key components:

1. Granting: Stock options are typically granted to employees as part of their compensation packages. The company grants the employee the right to purchase a certain number of shares in the future.

2. Exercise Price: The exercise price, also known as the strike price, is the predetermined price at which the employee can buy the company's stock when exercising the option.

3. Vesting: Stock options often have a vesting period, which is the duration of time an employee must wait before they can exercise their options. Vesting periods are designed to incentivize long-term commitment to the company and often occur over several years, with portions of the options becoming exercisable at specific intervals.

4. Exercising: When an employee decides to exercise their stock options, they purchase the specified number of shares at the predetermined exercise price. This transaction can typically occur after the options have vested and within a specified exercise window.

5. Market Price: The market price of the company's stock at the time of exercising the option determines the potential profit. If the market price is higher than the exercise price, the

employee can buy the shares at a lower price and sell them at a profit. If the market price is lower than the exercise price, the employee may choose not to exercise the options.

6. Expiration: Stock options have an expiration date, usually several years after the grant date. If the options are not exercised before the expiration date, they become worthless.

It's important to note that the mechanisms of stock options can vary depending on the specific terms set by the company and the type of options being issued, such as incentive stock options (ISOs) or non-qualified stock options (NSOs). Additionally, taxation rules also apply when exercising stock options, and employees should consult with financial and tax advisors for guidance specific to their situation.

What is a Candlestick?

A candlestick is a visual style type of price chart used in technical analysis that displays the high, low, open, and closing prices of a stock for a specific period. Each candlestick represents a data set of the complete price action during **a selected time frame.**

Why are candlesticks important?

A Candlestick show you the 2-price action of a stock and they confirm volume, buying pressure, and selling pressure.

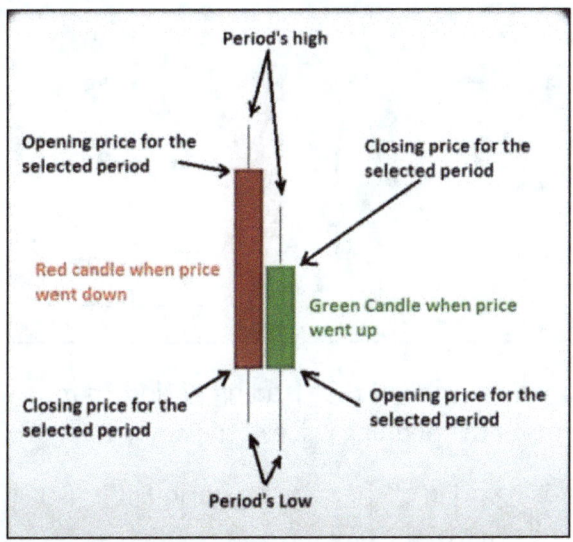

Bullish Candle Stock goes up:

A bullish candle says that within that predetermined time period, (whether it was 3 min, 5 min, 15 min, 30 min, 1 hour, 1 day, etc.), the buyers took control of most of it. To be a GREEN candle, the close (the closing price of that trading period) within that trading period has to be higher ↑ than the open (the opening price of that trading period). The difference between the close and open is called the body . The lines above the close and open are called shadows. The high represents the highest price of that trading period. The low c represents the lowest price of that trading period.

Bearish Candle- Stock goes down:

A bearish candle says that within that predetermined time period, (whether it was 3 min, 5 min, 15 min, 30 min, 1 hour etc.), the sellers z took control. To be a RED candle, the close within that trading period was lower ↓ than the open.

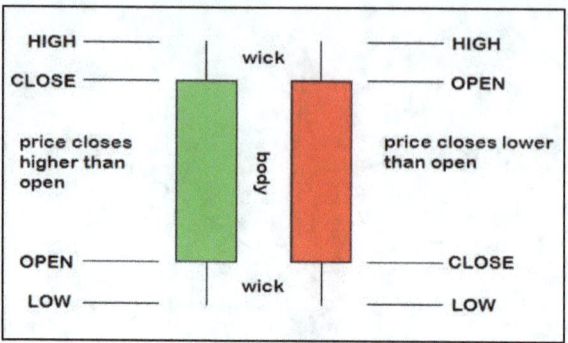

Open - the opening price of that trading period. In most cases this is spoken in terms of the opening price of the day.

Close - the closing price of that trading period. It it usually associated with the closing price of the day.

High - the highest price of that trading period. This is usually associated with the highest price that a stock reached during a day.

Low - the lowest price of that trading period. This is usually associated with the lowest price that stock reaches during the day.

Body: This body indicates the price range between the open and close of that day's trading. When the body is filled in or black, it means the close was lower than the open. If the real body is empty, it means the close was higher than the open.

Key Takeaways

1. Candlestick charts are used by traders to determine possible price movement based on past patterns.
2. Candlesticks are useful when trading as they show four price points (open, close, high, and low) throughout the period of the trader specifies.
3. Many algorithms are based on the same price information shown in candlestick charts.
4. Trading is often dictated by emotion, which can be read in candlestick charts.

How to read candlesticks and candlestick patterns

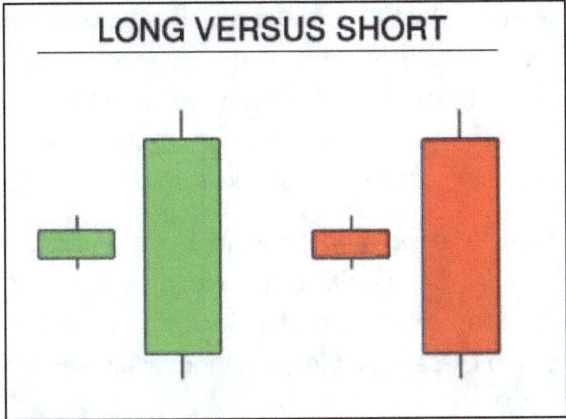

Long VS Short Bodies: Usually the longer the body is, the more intense the buying or selling pressure.

Short Green Candle: indicates that buying pressure is decreasing. This also shows that buying barely rose above the open of that period

Long Green Candle: The longer the green candle is, the further the close is above the open. This shows the prices advanced significantly and buyers were aggressive. Long green candles can mark as potential support levels after a long decline.

Short Red Candle: Short red candles show low selling pressure, and the prices drop just a little under the opening price. Short red candles can signal selling pressure is starting to weaken.

Long Red Candle: Long red candles indicate strong selling pressure. The longer the red candle is, the further the close is below the open. This means that prices declined significantly from the open and the sellers were very aggressive

For more details on learning about candle sticks and different types of patterns, I highly recommend doing research on *YouTube*, or reading *"Candlestick Charting for Dummies"*

Option Pricing & Valuation

Option pricing and valuation are essential aspects of understanding the value of stock options. Several models are commonly used to calculate the theoretical price of options. The most well-known model is the Black-Scholes-Merton model, which provides a framework for pricing European-style options on stocks that pay no dividends.

The Black-Scholes-Merton model considers several factors, including the current stock price, the strike price, the time to expiration, the risk-free interest rate, the volatility of the stock price, and the dividends, if any. By plugging in these variables, the model calculates the fair value of the option.

Other models, such as the Binomial model, are used to price options with more complex features or under different assumptions. These models involve constructing a binomial tree that represents the possible price movements of the underlying stock and calculating the option value at each node.

Valuation of options considers the pricing model and considers additional factors such as market conditions, supply and demand dynamics, and investor sentiment. The perceived value of options can fluctuate based on factors such as changes in the stock price, volatility, interest rates, and time to expiration.

It's important to note that option pricing models provide estimates of fair value, but actual option prices can differ due to market forces and factors not accounted for in the models. Traders and investors often use option pricing models as guides, but market prices ultimately reflect the collective opinion of market participants.

When valuing options, it's advisable to consider the specific terms and conditions of the options, such as vesting periods, exercise windows, and any contractual restrictions that may affect their value. Additionally, tax implications and potential risks associated with options should also be considered. Professional financial advice and consultation with experts can be beneficial for accurate option pricing and valuation.

Intrinsic Value vs Time Value

When it comes to options, understanding the concepts of intrinsic value and time value is crucial.

1. **Intrinsic Value**: The intrinsic value of an option represents the amount by which the option is in-the-money (ITM) or the immediate value the option would have if it were to be exercised at the current moment. For call options, the intrinsic value is the difference between the current stock price and the strike price, while for put options, it is the difference between the strike price and the current stock price. If an option has no intrinsic value, it is considered out-of-the-money (OTM).

    » For example, if a stock is trading at $50, a call option with a strike price of $45 would have an intrinsic value of $5 (50 - 45). Similarly, a put option with a strike price of $55 would have an intrinsic value of $5 (55 - 50).

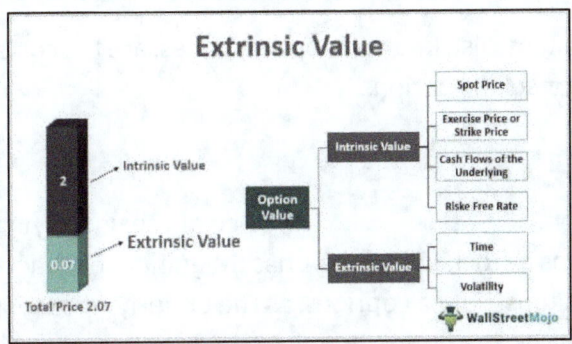

2. **Time Value**: Time value, also known as extrinsic value, is the additional value an option possesses beyond its intrinsic value. It represents the premium paid by an option buyer for the potential upside or downside of the underlying asset before the option's expiration. Time value is influenced by factors

such as time to expiration, implied volatility, interest rates, and market expectations.

» The longer the time until expiration, the higher the potential for the underlying asset's price to move in a favorable direction, and thus, the higher the time value. Conversely, as the expiration date approaches, the time value diminishes, eventually reaching zero at expiration.

» For instance, if a call option with an intrinsic value of $5 is trading at $8, the remaining $3 would be the time value component. This portion represents the market's expectation of potential future price movements and the option's flexibility.

Understanding the relationship between intrinsic value and time value is crucial for options traders and investors. In-the-money options have both intrinsic value and time value, at-the-money options have only time value, and out-of-the-money options have solely time value. The interplay between these two components affects the overall price of an option and the risk-reward dynamics associated with it.

Option premiums and factors affecting prices

Option premiums, also known as option prices, are the costs associated with buying or selling options.

Several factors influence the pricing of option premiums:

1. Underlying Asset Price: The price of the underlying asset, such as a stock or an index, has a significant impact on option premiums. For call options, as the underlying asset price increases, the option premium tends to rise, assuming other factors remain constant. Conversely, for put options, as the underlying asset price decreases, the option premium generally increases.

2. Strike Price: The strike price is the predetermined price at which the option can be exercised. The relationship between

the strike price and the current price of the underlying asset affects the option premium. In general, for call options, as the strike price gets closer to the current price of the underlying asset, the option premium increases. For put options, as the strike price moves further away from the current price, the option premium tends to rise.

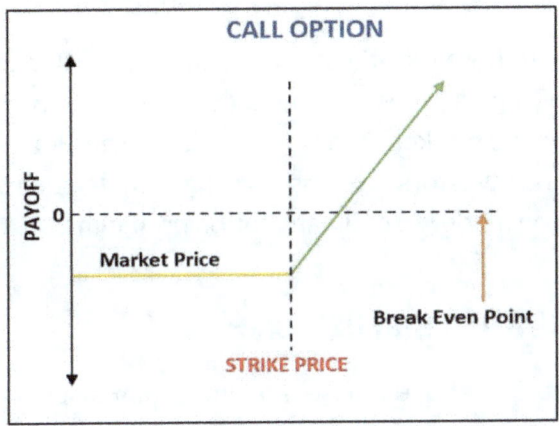

3. **Time to Expiration:** The time remaining until the option's expiration is a crucial factor in determining option premiums. Generally, as the time to expiration increases, option premiums tend to be higher due to the increased potential for the underlying asset's price to move favorably. However, as the expiration date approaches, the time value component diminishes, reducing the option premium.

4. **Volatility:** Volatility refers to the magnitude of price fluctuations in the underlying asset. Higher volatility generally leads to higher option premiums due to the increased potential for large price swings. Volatility is commonly measured by implied volatility, which represents the market's expectation of future price volatility. When implied volatility rises, option premiums tend to increase, and vice versa.

5. **Interest Rates:** Interest rates impact option pricing through their effect on the cost of carrying the underlying asset. Generally, higher interest rates result in higher option

premiums, especially for longer-term options, as the cost of holding the asset increases.

6. Dividends: For stocks that pay dividends, the timing and number of dividends can affect option premiums, particularly for call options. A higher dividend amount or a closer dividend payment date can decrease the option premium, as it reduces the expected future price appreciation of the stock.

It's important to note that these factors interact with each other and can have varying degrees of influence depending on the specific circumstances and market conditions. Option pricing is a complex field, and traders and investors often use pricing models, such as the Black-Scholes-Merton model, to estimate option premiums.

Option expiration and exercise

Option expiration and exercise are important aspects of options trading. Let's explore each concept:

1. Option Expiration: Every option has an expiration date, which is the predetermined date when the option contract ceases to be valid. After the expiration date, the option becomes worthless and cannot be traded or exercised. Expiration dates are typically standardized and occur on specific days, such as the third Friday of the month for most equity options in the United States.

2. Exercise: Exercising an option refers to the act of utilizing the rights granted by the option contract. When an option is exercised, the option holder (buyer) exercises their right to buy or sell the underlying asset at the predetermined strike price.

   ≫ Call Options: If an investor holds a call option, they can exercise it by buying the underlying asset at the strike price. This is typically done when the market price of the underlying asset is higher than the strike price, allowing the option holder to profit from the price difference.

» **Put Options:** If an investor holds a put option, they can exercise it by selling the underlying asset at the strike price. This is usually done when the market price of the underlying asset is lower than the strike price, enabling the option holder to profit from the price difference.

» It's important to note that the decision to exercise an option is solely at the discretion of the option holder. They may choose not to exercise the option if it is not profitable or if they prefer to close their position by selling the option contract itself.

3. **American-style vs. European-style Options:** Options can be classified as either American-style or European-style, depending on their exercise provisions.

» American-style options can be exercised by the option holder at any time before the expiration date. This gives the holder more flexibility since they can exercise the option when it is most advantageous.

» European-style options, on the other hand, can only be exercised at expiration. The holder must wait until the expiration date to exercise the option if they choose to do so.

» Most equity options traded in the United States are American-style, while many index options are European-style.

It's important for options traders and investors to be mindful of the expiration dates and understand the implications of exercising options. It is recommended to review the specific terms and conditions of the options contract, consult with financial advisors, and consider the market conditions and potential risks before making any decisions regarding exercise or allowing options to expire.

CHAPTER 3
Option Strategies for Beginners

Long Calls and Puts

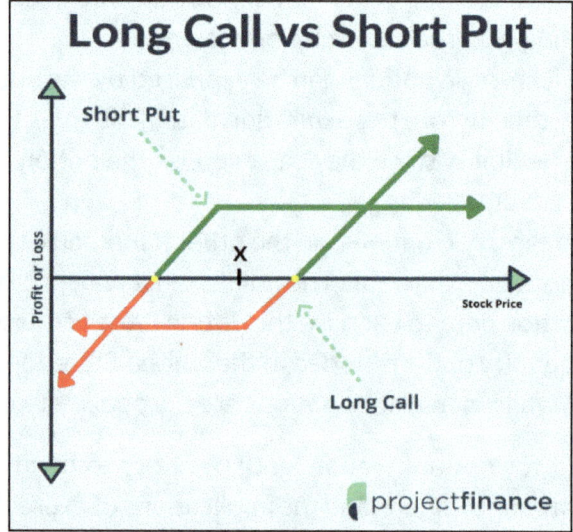

Long calls and puts are investment strategies used in options trading. Here's what they mean:

1. **Long Call:** When you have a long call position, it means you've purchased a call option. A call option gives you the right, but not the obligation, to buy an underlying asset (such as stocks, commodities, or currencies) at a specific price (the strike price) within a certain timeframe. By going long on a call option, you expect the price of the underlying asset to rise, as that would allow you to potentially profit from the option.

2. **Long Put:** On the other hand, having a long-put position means you've bought a put option. A put option gives you the right, but not the obligation, to sell an underlying asset at a specific price within a certain timeframe. By going long on a put option, you anticipate that the price of the underlying asset will decrease. This strategy allows you to potentially profit from the option if the asset's value falls below the strike price.

Both long calls and long puts can be used as speculative strategies to profit from price movements in the underlying asset. However, they can also be used as hedging tools to protect an existing investment position or portfolio. It's important to understand the risks and rewards associated with options trading and consider factors such as market conditions, volatility, and your investment goals before employing these strategies.

Covered Calls

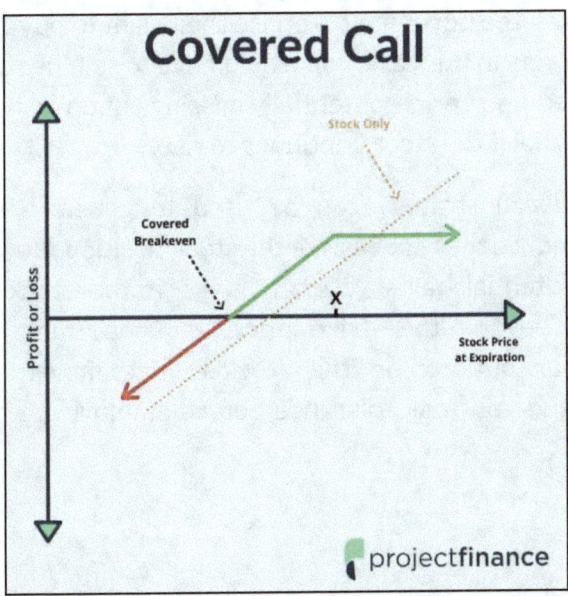

A covered call is an options strategy that involves holding a long position in an underlying asset (such as stocks) and simultaneously selling a call option on that asset. Here's how it works:

1. **Long Stock Position:** To implement a covered call strategy, you must first own the underlying asset, typically stocks. By having a long stock position, you benefit from any potential price appreciation of the stock.

2. **Selling Call Options:** Once you own the stock, you sell call options on those shares. Each call option represents the right, but not the obligation, for the buyer to purchase the underlying asset at a predetermined price (strike price) within a specific time period.

3. **Generating Income:** By selling the call options, you receive a premium (the amount the buyer pays for the option). This premium provides you with additional income on top of any dividends or capital gains from the stock itself.

4. **Obligation to Sell:** If the price of the underlying stock rises above the strike price of the call option before the option expires, the buyer may exercise their right to buy the shares from you. In this case, you would have to sell the shares at the agreed-upon price, potentially missing out on further upside potential if the stock continues to rise.

The covered call strategy can be used to generate income and potentially reduce the cost basis of the stock position. However, it also limits the potential gains you can make if the stock price rises significantly beyond the strike price. It's important to carefully consider your outlook on the stock's price movement, market conditions, and your risk tolerance before employing a covered call strategy.

Cash Secured Puts

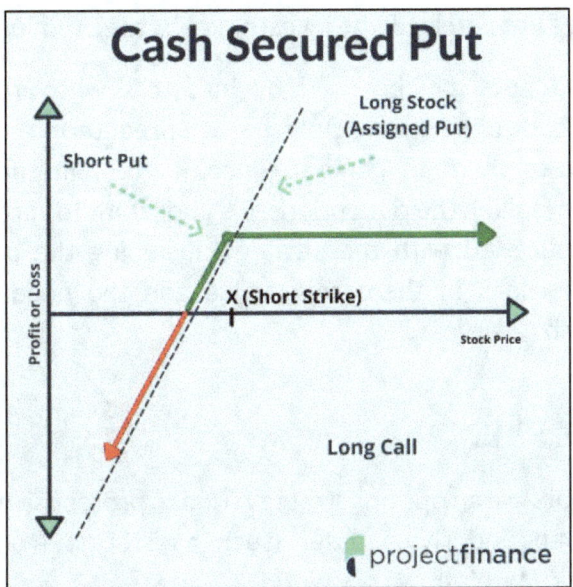

Cash-secured puts are an options strategy where an investor sells put options while setting aside enough cash to purchase the underlying asset if the options are exercised. Here's how it works:

1. Selling Put Options: The investor sells put options on a specific underlying asset (such as stocks) at a predetermined price (strike price) within a specified period. By selling the put options, the investor receives a premium from the buyer of the options.

2. Cash Reserves: To secure the puts, the investor sets aside sufficient cash in their account to cover the potential purchase of the underlying asset. This cash acts as collateral and ensures that the investor has enough funds to buy the assets at the strike price if the options are exercised.

3. Obligation to Buy: If the price of the underlying asset falls below the strike price and the put options are exercised by the buyer, the investor is obligated to buy the asset at the strike price. By setting aside cash, the investor has the means to fulfill this obligation.

4. **Premium as Income:** The premium received from selling the put options provides the investor with income. If the options expire unexercised, the investor keeps the premium as profit.

Cash-secured puts can be used by investors who are willing to potentially acquire the underlying asset at a predetermined price. This strategy allows them to generate income through the premiums received from selling the put options. It's important to carefully assess the risks associated with the strategy, including the potential for significant declines in the asset's value and the need to allocate sufficient cash reserves.

Protective Puts

Protective puts are an options strategy used to protect an existing long position in an underlying asset (such as stocks) from potential downside risk. Here's how they work:

1. **Long Position:** The investor already holds a long position in the underlying asset, meaning they own the asset with the expectation of price appreciation.
2. **Buying Put Options:** To protect against potential losses, the investor purchases put options on the same underlying asset. Each put option gives the investor the right, but not the obligation, to sell the asset at a specified price (strike price) within a specific time period.
3. **Hedging Against Downside Risk:** If the price of the underlying asset declines, the put options increase in value. This provides the investor with the ability to sell the asset at the strike price, limiting their potential losses.
4. **Cost of Protection:** Buying put options as a protective measure involves paying a premium for the options. This cost is a form of insurance against downside risk, similar to paying for an insurance policy.

By implementing a protective put strategy, investors can limit their potential losses on an existing long position in the underlying asset. If the asset's price decreases significantly, the gains from the put options can offset the losses in the underlying asset. However, if the asset's price remains stable or increases, the cost of the put options becomes an expense.

It's important to carefully consider the cost of the put options, the investor's risk tolerance, and the anticipated market conditions before implementing a protective put strategy.

Bullish and Bearish Spreads

Bullish and bearish spreads are options trading strategies used to take advantage of expected price movements in the underlying asset. Let's explore both:

1. Bullish Spread: - Call Spread: A bullish call spread involves buying a call option with a lower strike price and simultaneously selling a call option with a higher strike price. This strategy is used when the investor expects the price of the underlying asset to rise moderately. The goal is to profit from the price increase while minimizing the upfront cost of buying the call option. - Put Spread: A bullish put spread involves selling a put option with a higher strike price and simultaneously buying a put option with a lower strike price. This strategy is used when the investor expects the price of the underlying asset to rise slightly or remain stable. It allows the investor to profit from the premium received from selling the put option while limiting potential losses with the purchased put option.

2. Bearish Spread: - Put Spread: A bearish put spread involves buying a put option with a higher strike price and simultaneously selling a put option with a lower strike price. This strategy is used when the investor expects the price of the underlying asset to decline moderately. It allows the investor to profit from the price decrease while offsetting the cost of buying the put option. - Call Spread: A bearish call

spread involves selling a call option with a lower strike price and simultaneously buying a call option with a higher strike price. This strategy is used when the investor expects the price of the underlying asset to decline slightly or remain stable. It enables the investor to profit from the premium received from selling the call option while limiting potential losses with the purchased call option.

Both bullish and bearish spreads can be employed to manage risk, reduce upfront costs, and potentially increase the probability of profit. However, it's important to consider factors such as the expected price movement, market conditions, volatility, and the investor's risk tolerance before implementing these strategies.

CHAPTER 4
Advanced Option Trading Strategies

Iron Condors

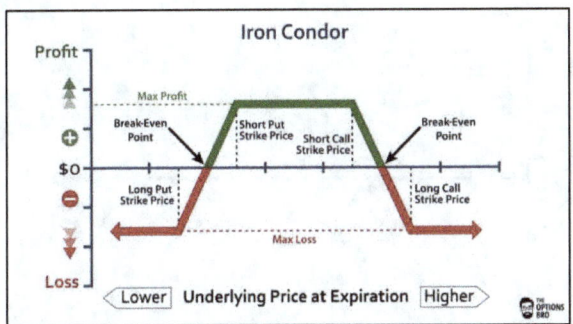

Iron condors are options trading strategies that involve the simultaneous buying and selling of call and put options with different strike prices. This strategy is used to profit from low volatility in the underlying asset.

An iron condor consists of four options trades: selling an out-of-the-money (OTM) call option, buying a further OTM call option, selling an OTM put option, and buying a further OTM put option. The difference in strike prices between the options establishes a range within which the trader expects the underlying asset's price to stay.

The goal of an iron condor is for the options to expire worthless, allowing the trader to keep the premiums collected when initially opening the position. It's a popular strategy when the trader believes that the underlying asset's price will remain relatively stable or trade within a specific range.

Iron condors can be complex and involve risk. It's important to have a good understanding of options trading and the associated risks before employing this strategy. Consulting with a financial advisor or professional is recommended for personalized guidance.

Butterfly Spreads

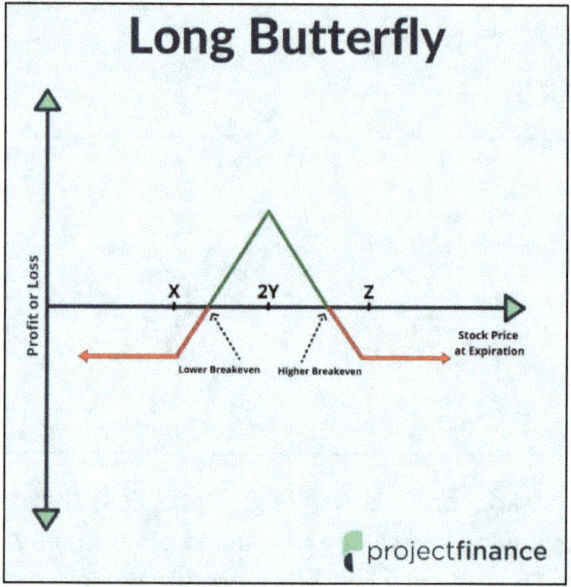

Butterfly spreads are options trading strategies that involve the combination of multiple options contracts with the same expiration date but different strike prices. They are named butterfly spreads because the risk profile of the strategy resembles the shape of a butterfly's wings.

A butterfly spread consists of three options trades: buying one option with a lower strike price, selling two options with a middle strike price, and buying another option with a higher strike price. The middle strike price is typically equidistant from the lower and higher strike prices.

The goal of a butterfly spread is to profit from a limited range of prices at expiration. The maximum profit is achieved if the underlying asset's price is at the middle strike price at expiration. The strategy is designed to take advantage of low volatility, and the risk is limited to the initial investment made to enter the trade.

Butterfly spreads can be used in different market scenarios, including when the trader expects the underlying asset's price to remain relatively stable or trade within a specific range. They can be constructed using either call options or put options, depending on the trader's market outlook.

As with any options strategy, it's important to understand the risks involved and have a good grasp of options trading concepts before using butterfly spreads. Consulting with a financial advisor or professional can provide personalized guidance based on your specific circumstances and market outlook.

Calendar Spread

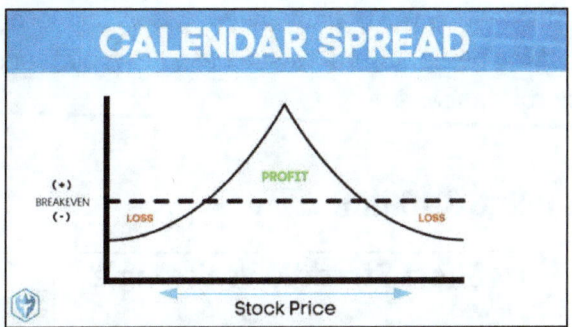

Calendar spreads, also known as time spreads or horizontal spreads, are options trading strategies that involve the simultaneous purchase and sale of options contracts with the same strike price but different expiration dates.

In a calendar spread, the trader buys a longer-term option and sells a shorter-term option. The idea behind this strategy is to take advantage of the time decay or theta decay of options. The shorter-term option typically has a higher rate of time decay compared to the longer-term option.

The goal of a calendar spread is to profit from the difference in time decay rates between the two options. If the underlying asset's price remains relatively stable and doesn't move significantly, the shorter-term option will lose value faster than the longer-term option. As a result, the trader can potentially profit from the decline in the shorter-term option's value while holding onto the longer-term option.

Calendar spreads can be constructed using either call options or put options, depending on the trader's market outlook. They are often used when the trader expects the underlying asset's price to remain near the strike price, resulting in the maximum profit potential for the strategy.

It's important to note that calendar spreads have limited profit potential and are subject to risks, such as changes in implied volatility and the price movement of the underlying asset. As with any options strategy, understanding the mechanics and risks involved is crucial. Seeking guidance from a financial advisor or professional is recommended for personalized advice based on your specific trading goals and risk tolerance.

Straddles and Strangles

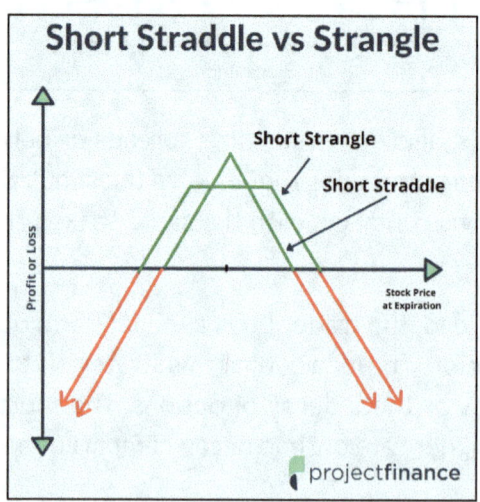

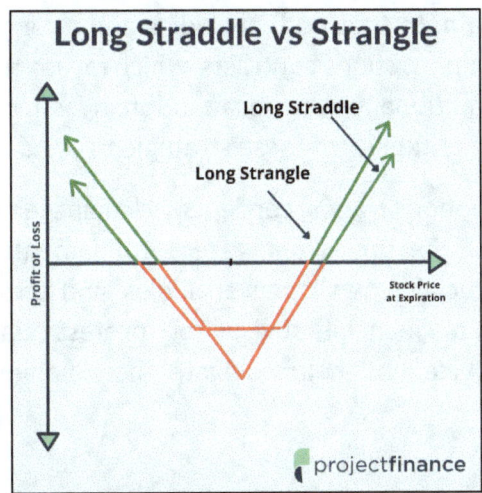

Straddles and strangles are options trading strategies that involve the simultaneous purchase of both a call option and a put option on the same underlying asset.

A straddle involves buying both a call option and a put option with the same strike price and expiration date. The expectation behind a straddle is that the underlying asset's price will experience a significant move, either upwards or downwards. The trader profits if the price moves enough to cover the combined cost of the options premiums.

On the other hand, a strangle is like a straddle but with different strike prices. It involves buying an out-of-the-money (OTM) call option and an OTM put option, both with the same expiration date. The strike price of the put option is typically lower than the call option. The expectation with a strangle is still a significant price move, but the trader doesn't necessarily expect the move to be as substantial as with a straddle.

Both straddles and strangles can be used when traders anticipate increased volatility or an upcoming event that could cause significant price fluctuations in the underlying asset. These strategies allow traders to profit from such price movements, regardless of whether the price goes up or down.

It's important to note that both straddles and strangles involve the purchase of multiple options contracts, which means they have higher upfront costs. Additionally, time decay and changes in implied volatility can impact the profitability of these strategies.

Understanding options trading concepts, risk management, and having a good grasp of the underlying asset's fundamentals and market conditions is crucial when using straddles and strangles. Seeking guidance from a financial advisor or professional can provide personalized advice and help navigate the complexities of these strategies.

Diagonal Spreads

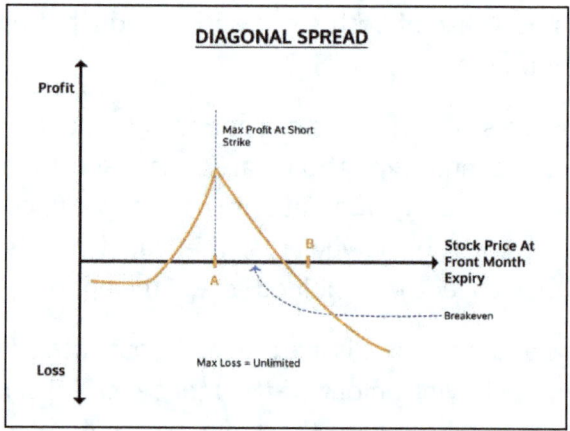

A diagonal spread is an options trading strategy that involves the simultaneous purchase and sale of options contracts with different strike prices and expiration dates. It combines elements of both vertical spreads and calendar spreads.

In a diagonal spread, the trader typically buys a longer-term option with a higher strike price and sells a shorter-term option with a lower strike price. The key difference between a diagonal spread and a vertical spread is that the expiration dates of the options are different, creating a diagonal shape on the options chain.

The goal of a diagonal spread is to take advantage of both time decay and price movement. The trader benefits from the time decay of the shorter-term option while still having exposure to potential price movements through the longer-term option. This strategy can be used when the trader expects the underlying asset's price to move moderately in a certain direction over time.

Diagonal spreads offer flexibility in adjusting the position by rolling the shorter-term option to a later expiration date or a different strike price. This adjustment allows the trader to manage risk and potentially profit from changes in market conditions.

It's important to note that diagonal spreads involve multiple options contracts and complex risk profiles. Understanding options trading concepts, such as time decay, implied volatility, and the relationship between strike prices and expiration dates, is crucial when implementing diagonal spreads.

As with any options strategy, there are risks involved, and it's recommended to consult with a financial advisor or professional who can provide personalized guidance based on your specific goals, risk tolerance, and market outlook.

CHAPTER 5

Risk Management and Position Sizing

Importance of Risk management

Risk management is of utmost importance in any financial endeavor, including trading and investing. It involves identifying, assessing, and mitigating risks to protect capital and achieve long-term success. Here are a few key reasons why risk management is crucial:

For Example: if you start out with $1000, the best practice is to only use **20%** ($200) of your funds per trade. A lot of beginners blow up their accounts by going all in on a trade, then end up losing hope on trading. Remember consistency is key and trading is not an overnight get rich scheme.

1. Capital Preservation: Effective risk management helps preserve capital by minimizing losses and protecting against adverse market movements. By implementing risk control measures, such as setting stop-loss orders or position sizing limits, traders and investors can limit the potential damage caused by unfavorable events.
2. Consistency: Consistency in trading or investing performance is vital for long-term success. Risk management ensures that losses are controlled and kept within acceptable limits, allowing for a more stable and predictable return profile over time. It helps avoid large drawdowns that can significantly hinder portfolio growth.

3. **Emotional Discipline:** Proper risk management helps maintain emotional discipline in decision-making. By having predefined risk parameters, traders and investors can prevent impulsive actions driven by fear or greed. This reduces the likelihood of making irrational or emotionally driven investment choices.

4. **Adaptability to Changing Market Conditions:** The financial markets are dynamic and subject to various uncertainties. Effective risk management strategies enable traders and investors to adapt to changing market conditions. By continuously monitoring and adjusting risk exposures, they can respond to evolving trends, volatility, and other market factors.

5. **Long-Term Sustainability:** Successful trading and investing require a long-term perspective. By managing risks effectively, individuals can ensure the sustainability of their strategies over an extended period. It helps avoid catastrophic losses that could wipe out an account or portfolio, allowing for continued participation and growth in the market.

Overall, risk management is an essential aspect of financial decision-making. It provides a structured approach to protect against downside risks, promote consistent performance, and enhance the likelihood of achieving long-term goals. It is prudent for individuals to develop and implement robust risk management practices as part of their trading or investment strategies.

Determining Risk Tolerance

Determining your risk tolerance is a crucial step in managing your investments and making informed financial decisions. Risk tolerance refers to your willingness and ability to endure fluctuations in the value of your investments and withstand potential losses. Here are some factors to consider when assessing your risk tolerance:

1. **Financial Goals:** Consider your financial goals, both short-term and long-term. Are you saving for retirement, a down

payment on a house, or funding a child's education? The time horizon and importance of these goals can influence your risk tolerance. Longer-term goals may allow for a higher risk tolerance, while shorter-term goals may call for a more conservative approach.

2. Time Horizon: Your investment time horizon is an important consideration. The longer your time horizon, the more time you have to recover from market downturns. If you have a longer time horizon, you may be more willing to tolerate short-term fluctuations and invest in potentially higher-risk assets.

3. Financial Situation: Assess your current financial situation, including income, expenses, debt, and available savings. A stable financial position with ample emergency funds and low debt can typically afford a higher risk tolerance. Conversely, if you have limited savings or high financial obligations, you may opt for a more conservative risk approach.

4. Knowledge and Experience: Consider your knowledge and experience with investing. Understanding different investment vehicles, risks associated with various asset classes, and market dynamics can help you make more informed decisions. If you are new to investing, you may initially have a lower risk tolerance until you gain more confidence and knowledge.

5. Emotional Resilience: Evaluate your emotional resilience and ability to handle market volatility. Some individuals are more comfortable with market fluctuations and can ride out short-term losses without feeling significant stress. Others may be more risk-averse and prefer a conservative approach to avoid emotional distress.

It's essential to strike a balance between risk and reward that aligns with your personal circumstances and comfort level. Understanding your risk tolerance can guide you in selecting appropriate investment strategies and asset allocations. However, it's recommended to consult with a financial advisor who can provide personalized guidance and help assess your risk tolerance based on your specific situation and investment objectives.

Stop Losses

Stop losses are risk management tools used in trading to help mitigate potential losses. A stop loss order is an instruction placed with a broker to sell a security if it reaches a specified price level, known as the stop price. It is designed to limit an investor's downside risk by automatically triggering a sale when the price falls to or below the predetermined stop price.

Here are a few key points to understand about stop losses:

1. Loss Limitation: The primary purpose of a stop loss is to limit potential losses on a trade. By setting a stop price, you establish a point at which you are willing to exit a position if the price moves against you. This can help protect your capital and prevent significant losses in case the market moves unfavorably.

2. Automation: Stop loss orders are executed automatically once the stop price is reached or breached. This eliminates the need for constant monitoring of positions and allows you to have predetermined risk management measures in place, even if you are unable to actively watch the market.

3. Market Volatility Considerations: It's important to consider the volatility of the market and the specific security when setting a stop loss. Placing a stop loss too close to the current price may result in frequent triggering of the order due to minor price fluctuations, potentially leading to premature exits. On the other hand, setting the stop loss too far away may expose you to larger potential losses.

4. Execution and Slippage: While stop loss orders aim to sell at or near the stop price, it's important to note that execution may not always occur precisely at the specified price. Market conditions, order size, and liquidity can impact the execution

price, potentially resulting in slippage, where the actual sale price differs from the stop price.

5. Individual Risk Tolerance: The determination of stop loss levels should be based on an individual's risk tolerance and trading strategy. Some traders may prefer tighter stop losses to limit risk, while others may use wider stop losses to allow for more significant price fluctuations. It's essential to align stop loss levels with your risk tolerance, trading plan, and overall investment objectives.

Remember that stop losses are risk management tools, but they are not foolproof and do not guarantee that losses will be completely avoided. Market conditions, gaps in pricing, and other factors can impact the execution of stop loss orders. It's important to understand the limitations and potential risks associated with stop losses and consider them as part of a comprehensive risk management strategy in your trading approach.

Setting Stop losses

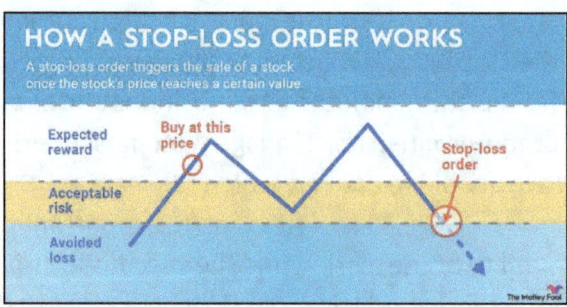

Setting stop losses involves determining the appropriate level at which to place the stop order in order to manage risk effectively. Here are some considerations for setting stop losses:

1. Support and Resistance Levels: Analyze price charts and identify key support and resistance levels. These levels represent areas where the price has historically shown strong buying or selling pressure. Placing a stop loss slightly below

support (for long positions) or above resistance (for short positions) can help protect against potential breakdowns or breakouts.

2. **Volatility and Average True Range (ATR):** Consider the volatility of the security you are trading. Volatile assets may require wider stop losses to account for larger price swings, while less volatile assets may have tighter stop losses. Average True Range (ATR) is a commonly used indicator that measures a security's volatility and can help determine an appropriate stop loss level based on recent price movements.

3. **Risk-Reward Ratio:** Assess the desired risk-reward ratio for your trades. Determine how much you are willing to risk on a trade relative to the potential reward. This ratio can help guide you in setting the distance between your entry price and stop loss level. For example, if you aim for a 2:1 risk-reward ratio, your stop loss level should be set at a distance where the potential profit is twice the potential loss.

4. **Time Frame and Trading Strategy:** Consider your trading time frame and strategy. Short-term traders may use tighter stop losses to quickly exit losing trades, while longer-term traders may use wider stop losses to allow for more significant price fluctuations. Align the stop loss level with your trading strategy and the time frame in which you expect the trade to play out.

5. **Account Size and Risk Tolerance:** Take into account your account size and risk tolerance. Smaller accounts may require tighter stop losses to limit risk exposure, while larger accounts may allow for wider stop losses. Assess your personal risk tolerance and adjust stop losses accordingly to ensure they align with your comfort level.

Remember that setting stop losses is a personal decision and should be based on your individual circumstances, trading strategy, and risk tolerance. It's important to regularly review and adjust stop loss levels as market conditions change and to follow risk management principles consistently. Additionally, consider combining stop losses with other risk management techniques, such as position sizing and diversification, to create a comprehensive risk management plan for your trading activities.

Position Sizing Strategies

Position sizing strategies are methods used to determine the appropriate size or allocation of capital to allocate to a specific trade or investment. Proper position sizing is crucial for managing risk and optimizing portfolio performance. Here are a few common position sizing strategies:

1. **Fixed Dollar Amount:** This approach involves allocating a fixed dollar amount or percentage of your capital to each trade or investment. For example, you may decide to risk no more than 2% of your total portfolio value on any single trade. This strategy ensures consistent risk exposure across different trades, regardless of the size of each position.

2. **Fixed Percentage of Capital:** With this strategy, you allocate a fixed percentage of your total capital to each trade. For instance, you may choose to risk 5% of your capital on each trade. As your account balance fluctuates, the position size adjusts accordingly. This strategy allows for dynamic allocation based on the available capital but maintains a consistent risk level.

3. **Volatility-based Position Sizing:** This approach takes into account the volatility of the security or market being traded. It involves adjusting position sizes based on measures like Average True Range (ATR) or standard deviation. Higher volatility may warrant a smaller position size to account for larger potential price swings, while lower volatility may allow for a larger position size.

4. **Kelly Criterion:** The Kelly Criterion is a mathematical formula that helps determine the optimal position size based on the probability of success and the potential reward-to-risk ratio. It takes into account the trader's win rate and average

profit/loss per trade. The Kelly Criterion suggests position sizes that maximize long-term portfolio growth while considering risk.

5. Risk Parity: Risk parity aims to allocate capital based on risk rather than the dollar amount invested. It involves assigning a target risk level for each position, which can be measured using metrics such as Value at Risk (VaR) or expected volatility. The position sizes are then adjusted to achieve equal risk contribution from each position in the portfolio.

Remember that position sizing strategies should be aligned with your risk tolerance, trading/investment strategy, and overall financial goals. It's important to consider factors such as account size, risk appetite, and market conditions when implementing a position sizing strategy. Regularly reviewing and adjusting position sizes based on changes in account balance, market conditions, and risk factors is also essential for effective risk management and portfolio performance.

CHAPTER 6

Fundamental and Technical Analysis for Options Trading

Fundamental and technical analysis are both important tools used in options trading.

Fundamental analysis involves evaluating the underlying factors that can impact the value of an asset. This analysis considers factors such as financial statements, industry trends, economic indicators, and company news. Fundamental analysis helps traders determine the intrinsic value of an option by assessing the underlying asset's fundamentals.

On the other hand, technical analysis focuses on studying price patterns, trends, and market indicators to predict future price movements. Traders who use technical analysis examine charts, patterns, and indicators like moving averages, support and resistance levels, and volume. This approach helps identify potential entry and exit points for options trading.

Combining both fundamental and technical analysis can provide a comprehensive approach to options trading. Fundamental analysis helps understand the long-term prospects and value of an underlying asset, while technical analysis provides insights into short-term price movements and timing of trades. Traders often use a combination of these approaches to make informed decisions and manage risks effectively in options trading.

Evaluating Stocks for Options Trading

When evaluating stocks for options trading, there are several key factors to consider. Here's a step-by-step guide on how to evaluate stocks for options trading:

1. **Understand the company:** Start by researching and understanding the company whose stock you are considering for options trading. Look into its financial health, business model, competitive advantage, management team, and growth prospects. This information will help you gauge the company's overall stability and potential.

2. **Analyze fundamental indicators:** Evaluate fundamental indicators such as earnings per share (EPS), revenue growth, profit margins, and debt levels. These indicators provide insights into the company's financial performance and stability. A strong fundamental foundation can increase the likelihood of favorable options trading outcomes.

3. **Assess industry and market trends:** Consider the broader industry and market trends that may impact the stock's performance. Evaluate factors such as market demand, competitive landscape, regulatory environment, and any

upcoming events or news that could influence the stock's price.

4. **Review technical indicators:** Utilize technical analysis techniques to examine the stock's price patterns, trends, and trading volume. Technical indicators like moving averages, support and resistance levels, and momentum oscillators can help identify potential entry and exit points for options trades.

5. **Volatility assessment:** Options trading heavily relies on volatility. Assess the historical and implied volatility of the stock. High volatility can offer more trading opportunities but may also carry higher risks. Evaluate the stock's volatility to align it with your trading strategy and risk tolerance.

6. **Options liquidity:** Ensure that the stock you choose for options trading has sufficient options liquidity. High liquidity ensures that there are enough buyers and sellers in the options market, allowing you to enter and exit positions easily at fair prices.

7. **Risk management:** Consider your risk tolerance and develop a risk management strategy. Determine appropriate strike prices, expiration dates, and option strategies that align with your risk-reward profile. Additionally, evaluate the potential risks associated with the stock, such as upcoming earnings announcements or regulatory changes.

By considering these factors and conducting thorough analysis, you can make informed decisions when evaluating stocks for options trading. It's essential to stay updated on market news and continuously monitor your positions to adapt to changing market conditions.

Analyzing Market trends and indicators

Analyzing market trends and indicators is a crucial aspect of evaluating investment opportunities. Here are some key steps to consider when analyzing market trends and indicators:

1. **Identify the market trend:** Determine whether the overall market is trending upward, downward, or moving sideways. This can be done by analyzing broad market indices, such as the S&P 500 or Dow Jones Industrial Average, or by examining sector-specific indices.

2. **Use technical analysis tools:** Utilize technical analysis tools to identify patterns, trends, and signals in price charts. Common technical indicators include moving averages, trendlines, support and resistance levels, and momentum oscillators like the Relative Strength Index (RSI) or Moving Average Convergence Divergence (MACD). These tools can help you understand the current market sentiment and potential future price movements.

3. **Assess market breadth:** Evaluate market breadth indicators, such as the Advance-Decline Line or the number of stocks making new highs or lows. Market breadth provides insights into the overall participation and strength of the market. A healthy market trend is typically supported by broad market participation.

4. **Monitor economic indicators:** Keep an eye on key economic indicators, such as GDP growth, inflation rates, interest rates, and employment data. These indicators can provide insights into the overall health of the economy and its potential impact on the market.

5. **Stay informed about news and events:** Stay updated on relevant news, corporate earnings releases, economic announcements, and geopolitical events that can influence market trends. News events can create volatility and impact market sentiment, leading to potential trading opportunities.

6. **Consider sentiment indicators:** Assess sentiment indicators, such as investor surveys, put-call ratios, or the Volatility Index (VIX). These indicators can provide insights into market sentiment, fear or greed levels, and potential contrarian trading opportunities.

7. Utilize historical data: Analyze historical market trends and patterns to gain insights into recurring market behaviors. This analysis can help identify potential support and resistance levels, seasonal patterns, or recurring market cycles.

Remember that analyzing market trends and indicators involves a combination of art and science. It's important to use multiple tools and indicators to get a comprehensive view of the market. Additionally, consider the limitations and potential biases of each indicator, and always validate your analysis with additional research and professional advice if needed.

Using volatility to your advantage

Volatility can be used to your advantage in various ways when it comes to trading and investing. Here are a few strategies that leverage volatility:

1. Volatility-based option strategies: Volatility plays a significant role in options pricing. By analyzing and anticipating changes in volatility, you can implement strategies such as buying or selling options to take advantage of price swings. For instance, if you expect increased volatility, you might consider purchasing options to benefit from potential larger price movements.

2. Volatility breakout trading: Volatility breakout strategies involve identifying periods of low volatility followed by anticipated increased volatility. Traders can enter positions when the price breaks out of a consolidation phase, aiming to capture potential significant price movements. This approach is often used in conjunction with technical indicators or chart patterns.

3. Volatility arbitrage: This strategy involves taking advantage of price discrepancies between different securities or derivative instruments that are influenced by volatility. Traders simultaneously enter long and short positions to

profit from relative mispricings caused by differing volatility levels.

4. **Volatility-based portfolio allocation:** Volatility can influence risk and return characteristics. By considering the volatility of different assets or asset classes, you can allocate your portfolio in a way that balances risk and potential returns. Lower volatility assets may be favored during uncertain times, while higher volatility assets might be suitable during periods of stability or growth.

5. **Volatility-based stop-loss orders:** Volatility can help determine appropriate stop-loss levels. By setting stop-loss orders based on volatility levels, you can potentially protect your positions from excessive downside risk. Adjusting stop-loss levels according to changes in volatility can help adapt to shifting market conditions.

It's important to note that while volatility can present opportunities, it also carries risks. Proper risk management, including position sizing, diversification, and understanding the potential impact of volatility on your trading strategy, is essential.

Additionally, it's recommended to stay updated on market news, economic events, and company-specific factors that can influence volatility. This information can help you make informed decisions and adjust your strategies accordingly.

Implementing Options Strategies based on Analysis

Implementing options strategies based on analysis involves utilizing your analysis of underlying assets, market trends, and volatility to construct and execute options trades. Here are a few examples of options strategies commonly employed:

1. **Long Call or Put:** If you anticipate a significant price move in an underlying asset, you can purchase a long call option (if bullish) or a long put option (if bearish). This strategy allows

you to profit from favorable price movements while limiting your downside risk to the premium paid.

2. Covered Call: This strategy involves holding a long position in an asset while simultaneously selling a call option on that same asset. By selling the call option, you collect premium income, which can help offset any potential losses in the underlying asset's value. This strategy is often used to generate additional income from a stock position.

3. Bull or Bear Spread: Spread strategies involve simultaneously buying and selling options with different strike prices or expiration dates. Bull spreads (e.g., bull call spread) are used when you expect a moderate upward move in the underlying asset, while bear spreads (e.g., bear put spread) are used for moderate downward moves. These strategies allow for limited risk and potential profit.

4. Straddle or Strangle: Straddle and strangle strategies are used when you anticipate significant price volatility but are uncertain about the direction. A straddle involves simultaneously buying a call option and a put option with the same strike price and expiration date. A strangle is similar, but the call and put options have different strike prices. These strategies aim to profit from sharp price moves, regardless of the direction.

5. Iron Condor: This strategy combines a bullish and bearish credit spread. It involves selling an out-of-the-money call spread and an out-of-the-money put spread simultaneously. The goal is to generate premium income while having a range within which the underlying asset's price should remain. This strategy is typically used in a relatively stable or range-bound market.

Remember to consider the potential risks and rewards of each strategy, including transaction costs and the impact of changes in volatility. It's crucial to fully understand the mechanics of each strategy and to carefully manage your positions by setting appropriate stop-loss orders or adjusting your trades as market conditions evolve.

Options trading involves risks, and it's advisable to consult with a financial advisor or engage in thorough research before implementing complex options strategies.

CHAPTER 7

Practical Tips for Successful Option Trading

Below are Few recommended trading platforms: An electronic trading platform that allows users to place orders for financial products over a network with a financial liaison. These products include products such as stocks, bonds, & currencies.

> » Robin Hood- (*Preferred for Swing & Leap Trading*)- Beginner's Recommended
> » Tasty Works-
> » Thinkorswim- (*Preferred for Day trading*)
> » WeBull- (*Preferred for Day Trading*)
> » E-Trade-
> » Vanguard-

Choosing the right options broker is crucial for your trading success. There are several factors to consider when selecting an options broker that best suits your needs and trading style. Here are some essential factors to consider:

Commission and Fees: Compare the commission and fees charged by different brokers for options trading. Look for brokers that offer competitive rates and consider how these costs may impact your overall trading profitability.

Platform and Technology: A user-friendly and reliable trading platform is essential for executing trades efficiently. Ensure that the broker's platform provides the necessary tools, charts, and data you need for options trading.

Option Chains and Research Tools: Options trading involves complex strategies, and access to robust research tools and option chains is vital. Check if the broker provides in-depth analysis, educational resources, and relevant market data.

Account Types and Minimums: Consider your budget and the minimum deposit required to open an account with the broker. Some brokers offer different account types based on the level of trading experience, each with varying features and benefits.

Customer Service: Good customer support can be crucial, especially for beginners. Look for brokers that offer responsive customer service through multiple channels, such as phone, email, and live chat.

Regulation and Security: Ensure that the options broker you choose is regulated by a reputable financial authority. Regulation provides an extra layer of security for your funds and ensures that the broker follows industry standards and rules.

Margin Requirements: If you plan to trade options using margin, pay attention to the margin requirements set by the broker. Different brokers may have varying margin rules, which can impact your trading strategies.

Mobile Trading: If you prefer to trade on the go, check if the broker offers a reliable mobile trading app with features that allow you to manage your options positions effectively.

Educational Resources: Especially for beginners, having access to educational resources can be invaluable. Look for brokers that provide webinars, tutorials, articles, and other educational materials to help you improve your options trading skills.

Availability of Options Contracts: Ensure that the broker offers a wide range of options contracts on various underlying assets. A diverse selection of options will provide more opportunities for your trading strategies.

Reviews and Reputation: Before making a final decision, check online reviews and the broker's reputation in the trading community. Feedback from other traders can give you insights into the broker's strengths and weaknesses.

Remember that your choice of an options broker should align with your specific trading goals, risk tolerance, and level of experience. It's essential to conduct thorough research and even test the broker's platform with a demo account before committing real funds. This way, you can ensure that the broker meets your requirements and helps you achieve your trading objectives.

Managing Emotions and Discipline

Managing emotions and maintaining discipline are essential aspects of successful trading and investing. Emotions can often cloud judgment and lead to impulsive decisions, while discipline helps you stick to your trading plan and make rational choices. Here are some tips for effectively managing emotions and maintaining discipline:

Create a Trading Plan: Develop a well-defined trading plan that outlines your goals, risk tolerance, entry and exit criteria, and position sizing. Having a plan in place can help you stay focused and reduce the influence of emotions on your trading decisions.

Stick to Your Strategy: Once you have a trading plan, follow it diligently. Avoid making impulsive decisions based on fear or greed. Consistently implementing your strategy can lead to more disciplined and successful trading.

Set Realistic Goals: Set achievable and realistic trading goals. Understand that trading is not a get-rich-quick scheme, and success may take time. Unrealistic expectations can lead to frustration and emotional trading. Once you've hit your daily goal, log out or close your computer to avoid temptation from overtrading.

Use Risk Management: Implement proper risk management techniques, such as setting stop-loss orders and not risking more than a certain percentage of your trading capital on any single trade. This can help protect your capital and reduce emotional stress during volatile market conditions.

Learn to Accept Losses: Losses are an inherent part of trading. Avoid getting emotionally attached to individual trades and accept that some will result in losses. Focus on the long-term performance of your trading strategy instead.

Avoid Overtrading: Trading excessively can lead to emotional exhaustion and impulsive decisions. Stick to your trading plan and avoid the temptation to make trades just for the sake of being active in the market. Avoid "(FOMO) Fair of Missing Out as much as possible. There will always be another successful trade that you can catch the next trading day.

Take Breaks: If you find yourself becoming emotional or stressed, take a step back from trading. Sometimes, taking a break can help clear your mind and prevent you from making irrational decisions.

Stay Informed: Stay up-to-date with market news and developments. Being well-informed can provide you with a sense of control and confidence in your trading decisions.

Maintain a Trading Journal: Keep a trading journal to track your trades, including the reasoning behind each trade and the emotions you experienced during the process. Regularly reviewing your journal can help you identify patterns and areas for improvement.

Practice Patience: Patience is a vital trait in trading. Wait for the right setups and opportunities to align with your trading plan, rather than forcing trades out of impatience.

Seek Support: Discuss your trading experiences and challenges with fellow traders or a mentor. Having a support system can provide valuable insights and encouragement during tough times.

Remember that managing emotions and maintaining discipline in trading is an ongoing process that requires self-awareness and practice. By prioritizing these aspects, you can improve your trading performance and increase your chances of long-term success.

Learning from Mistakes and Adapting Strategies

Learning from mistakes and adapting strategies are crucial steps for growth and improvement in trading and investing. Every trader, no matter their level of experience, will make mistakes at some point. The key is to recognize these mistakes, learn from them, and adjust your strategies accordingly. Here are some tips on how to effectively learn from mistakes and adapt your trading strategies:

Keep a Trading Journal: Maintaining a detailed trading journal is one of the best ways to learn from your mistakes. Record each trade, including the reasons for entering and exiting the trade, your emotions, and the outcome. Regularly review your journal to identify patterns of success and areas for improvement.

Analyze Losing Trades: When a trade results in a loss, don't simply dismiss it as a failure. Instead, examine the trade to understand what went wrong. Was there an error in your analysis or execution? Did you violate your trading plan? Identifying the reasons for the loss can help you avoid repeating the same mistakes.

Seek Feedback: If possible, seek feedback from experienced traders or mentors. They may offer valuable insights and point out blind spots that you may have missed.

Practice Self-Reflection: Take some time after each trading session to reflect on your performance. Consider your emotional state, decision-making process, and adherence to your trading plan. Honest self-reflection can lead to self-awareness and improved decision-making.

Adapt to Market Conditions: Markets are dynamic, and what works in one type of market may not be effective in another. Be open to adjusting your strategies based on changing market conditions, trends, and volatility.

Back test and Forward Test: Before implementing significant changes to your strategy, backtest it on historical data to see how it would have performed in the past. Then, forward test the modified strategy with a demo account to observe how it performs in real-time market conditions.

Avoid Revenge Trading: After a significant loss or mistake, it's common to feel the urge to "get back" at the market. This emotional reaction can lead to revenge trading, which often results in more losses. Recognize this tendency and take a break if needed to regain a clear mindset.

Stay Disciplined: While adapting your strategy is essential, ensure that you maintain discipline in your decision-making. Don't make impulsive changes or abandon your trading plan without proper analysis.

Continuously Educate Yourself: The financial markets are always evolving, and there is always more to learn. Stay committed to continuous education and seek to improve your trading skills and knowledge.

Be Patient and Persistent: Adapting your strategies and learning from mistakes is an ongoing process. Be patient with yourself and remain persistent in your efforts to improve.

Remember that successful traders are not immune to mistakes, but they are proactive in their approach to learning and adapting. By applying these principles, you can develop a more resilient and effective trading approach over time.

Resources for Ongoing Education and Research

Continuing education and research are essential for staying informed and improving your trading and investing skills. There are numerous resources available to help you expand your knowledge and keep up-to-date with the financial markets. Here are some valuable resources for ongoing education and research:

» **Financial News Websites:** Stay updated with the latest market news and developments through reputable financial news websites like Bloomberg, CNBC, Reuters, and Financial Times.

» **Investing and Trading Books:** There are many books written by experienced traders and investors that can provide valuable insights and knowledge. Some popular titles include "Market Wizards" by Jack D. Schwager, "The Intelligent Investor" by Benjamin Graham, and "Reminiscences of a Stock Operator" by Edwin Lefèvre.

» **Online Courses and Webinars:** Many online platforms offer courses and webinars on various trading and investing topics. Websites like Investopedia, Udemy, and Coursera have a wide range of courses taught by experts in the field.

» **Financial Magazines:** Subscribe to financial magazines like Barron's, Forbes, and The Economist, which offer in-depth analysis and market insights.

» **Trading Forums and Communities:** Participate in online trading forums and communities where traders share ideas, strategies, and experiences.

» **Financial Blogs:** Follow financial blogs written by respected experts and analysts. Blogs can provide valuable opinions and perspectives on market trends and specific assets.

» **Financial YouTube Channels and Podcasts:** There are many YouTube channels and podcasts focused on finance and investing. Some popular channels include Bloomberg, Real Vision Finance, and MarketWatch.

» **Technical Analysis Platforms:** If you are interested in technical analysis, platforms like TradingView provide a wealth of technical charts and tools, along with a community of traders sharing ideas.

» **Company Filings and Reports:** Access company filings and reports on the Securities and Exchange Commission (SEC) website or other financial data providers. These reports offer insights into a company's financial health and performance.

» **Economic Calendars:** Stay aware of upcoming economic events and announcements that can impact on the markets by using economic calendars like those provided by Investing.com or Forex Factory.

» **Financial Analysts and Experts on social media:** Follow reputable financial analysts, economists, and experts on social media platforms like Twitter for real-time market updates and insights.

» **Brokerage Research and Tools:** Some online brokerage platforms offer research reports, analyst ratings, and stock screeners that can aid in your research process.

Remember to always verify the credibility and reputation of the sources you use for research and education. Not all information found online is accurate or reliable, so it's essential to cross-reference information from multiple sources before making important trading or investment decisions. Continuous learning is a key factor in successful trading, so dedicating time and effort to ongoing education can significantly benefit your financial endeavors.

CHAPTER 8
Case Studies and Examples

Trade Examples for Different Strategies

Here are a few of my favorite trading strategies. Let's go through some trade examples for different trading strategies. Please note that these examples are for illustrative purposes only and not financial advice. Always do your research and consider your risk tolerance before making any trades.

Trend Following Strategy:

The trend following strategy involves identifying and following the prevailing market trend. Traders using this strategy aim to buy assets that are in an uptrend and sell assets that are in a downtrend.

Example: Let's say a trader notices that the price of a particular stock, XYZ Inc., has been steadily increasing over the past few months. The trader decides to implement a trend following strategy and buys shares of XYZ Inc. as the stock price continues to rise. The trader holds onto the position until there are clear signal that the uptrend is reversing, at which point they would sell their shares to lock in profits.

Mean Reversion Strategy:

The mean reversion strategy involves trading based on the assumption that prices will revert to their historical averages or a specific mean value after deviating from it.

Example: Suppose a trader identifies a stock that has been experiencing frequent price fluctuations. Whenever the price deviates significantly from its 50-day moving average, the trader executes a trade based on the expectation that the price will revert to the average. If the price is significantly above the moving average, the trader sells the stock, expecting it to fall back down to the average. Conversely, if the price is significantly below the moving average, the trader buys the currency pair, expecting it to rise back up to the average.

Breakout & Retest Strategy:

The breakout strategy involves trading based on the idea that when an asset's price breaks through a significant level of support or resistance, it will continue moving in the same direction, gaining momentum.

First is understanding **support and resistance area**. Resistance is a series of highs and "support" is a series of lows. Resistance is your ceiling and support is your floor.

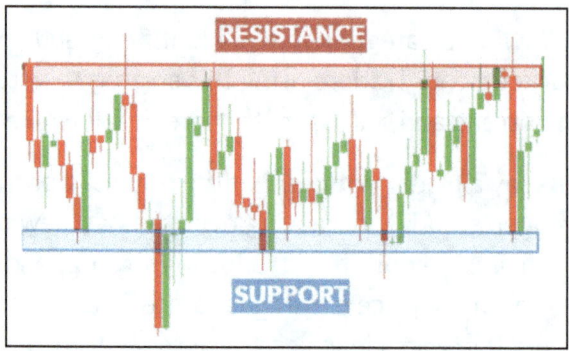

The Break and Retest strategy is a popular trading approach used by traders to capitalize on potential trend reversals or continuation after a significant breakout from a key level of support or resistance. This strategy combines elements of both breakout trading and pullback trading. The basic idea is to wait for a breakout, then observe whether the broken level is retested before entering a trade in the direction of the breakout.

Here are the steps involved in the Break and Retest strategy:

1. **Identify Key Support or Resistance Level:** First, you need to identify a significant support or resistance level on the price chart. This level should have historical importance and be recognized by other traders as well.

2. **Wait for Breakout:** Monitor the price action to see if the price convincingly breaks above (in case of resistance) or below (in case of support) the identified level. The breakout should ideally be accompanied by higher-than-average trading volume to validate its strength.

3. **Wait for Retest:** After the breakout, be patient and wait for the price to retest the broken level. In a valid break and retest scenario, the broken level should now act as the opposite (support turned resistance in a bearish breakout, or resistance turned support in a bullish breakout).

4. **Confirmation and Entry:** Once the retest occurs, observe how the price reacts to the former support/resistance level. If the price confirms the new role of the broken level (i.e., acts as resistance after a break of support or acts as support after a break of resistance) and shows signs of rejection, you may consider entering a trade in the direction of the breakout.

5. **Set Stop-Loss and Take-Profit:** As with any trading strategy, it's essential to manage risk. Set a stop-loss order just beyond the retested level to protect your position if the trade goes against you. Determine a take-profit level based on your risk-reward ratio or other technical indicators.

6. **Manage the Trade:** Once in the trade, monitor it closely and adjust your stop-loss and take-profit levels if necessary. Consider trailing your stop-loss to lock in profits as the price moves in your favor.

Remember that no trading strategy is foolproof, and there is always a risk of losses. It's crucial to practice proper risk management, use appropriate position sizing, and combine the Break and Retest strategy with other technical indicators or analysis methods to increase the probability of successful trades.

Additionally, like any trading strategy, the Break and Retest approach requires careful analysis and practice. It's a good idea to back test the strategy using historical price data and practice in a demo account before applying it to live trading.

Scalping Strategy:

Scalping is a high-frequency trading strategy where traders aim to make small profits from multiple quick trades throughout the day.

Example: A scalper focuses on the forex market and aims to profit from small price movements. They closely monitor stocks and enter and exit positions within minutes or even seconds. For instance, the trader might enter a long position on TSLA when they see a slight uptick in price and quickly exit the trade when they've made profit.

Remember, successful trading requires discipline, risk management, and continuous learning. It's essential to practice these strategies in a simulated environment or with small positions before applying them in live markets. Additionally, seek advice from professional financial advisors and always be aware of the risks involved in trading.

Trade Simulations and Back testing Tools

Trade simulations and back testing tools are essential for traders and investors to test their trading strategies and assess their historical performance before risking real capital in the markets. Here are some popular trade simulation and back testing tools:

TradingView (Most Recommended): Trading View is a popular web-based platform that provides interactive charts and technical analysis tools. It also offers a powerful back testing engine that allows users to test their trading strategies using historical price data for various asset classes.

First... You'll need to download the Trading View application. This is the app I use to draw patterns and analyze stocks. I usually use my iPad, iPhone, or laptop as well. Most of us have jobs or are on the go so it's best to use items that you carry with you on a daily basis.

Second, I would recommend using this stock screener website on a daily called FINVIZ.Com or Stockcharts.com for Candlestick patterns, top gainers, new highs, and new lows on the DOW, NASDAQ, and S&P 500.

Additionally, keep in mind that past performance is not indicative of future results, and live trading results may differ from back test results due to various factors like slippage, liquidity, and market conditions. Always validate your strategies in a live, but controlled, trading environment before committing significant capital.

Paper Trading

Paper trading, also known as simulated or virtual trading, is a practice used by traders and investors to test their trading strategies and gain experience without risking real money. It involves executing trades in a simulated environment that replicates the real market conditions, including price movements and order executions.

I highly recommend using "Webull" to start paper trading with everything you've learned so far.

Here's how paper trading works:

Simulated Trading Platform: To start paper trading, you need access to a simulated trading platform. Many online brokerage platforms offer paper trading accounts alongside their real trading accounts. These platforms provide you with virtual funds to use for trading in a risk-free environment.

Selecting Trading Instruments: In the paper trading platform, you can choose from various financial instruments, such as stocks, options, futures, forex, or cryptocurrencies, to practice trading. Ensure that the platform offers the same instruments you are interested in trading in real life.

Implementing Trading Strategies: Use the simulated funds to implement and test your trading strategies. You can follow the same trading rules, technical indicators, and risk management techniques as you would in real trading. This helps you gauge how your strategy would have performed in historical market conditions.

Tracking Performance: Keep track of your paper trading performance, including the number of trades made, profits, losses, and overall portfolio value. This analysis helps you evaluate the effectiveness of your strategies and identify areas for improvement.

Benefits of Paper Trading:

Risk-Free Learning: Paper trading allows you to gain experience and learn from both successful and unsuccessful trades without risking real money. It is an excellent way to practice and refine your trading skills.

Testing Strategies: You can test multiple trading strategies and determine which ones work best for your trading style without facing any financial consequences.

Familiarizing with the Platform: For beginners, paper trading helps in getting acquainted with the trading platform's features, order types, and charting tools.

Confidence Building: Successful paper trading can boost your confidence before you start trading with real money.

Eliminating Emotional Factors: Since there is no real money at stake, paper trading helps remove emotions from the trading process, allowing you to make objective decisions.

Remember that paper trading has its limitations, as it cannot fully replicate the real emotional and psychological aspects of live trading. When transitioning to real trading, start with a small amount of capital and implement proper risk management strategies to protect your investment.

Overall, paper trading is a valuable tool for traders of all levels, from beginners to experienced professionals, to refine their skills and build confidence in their trading strategies.

CHAPTER 9
Conclusion

In conclusion, paper trading is a highly beneficial practice for traders and investors who want to gain experience, test their trading strategies, and improve their skills without risking real money. By using a simulated trading platform with virtual funds, traders can replicate real market conditions and execute trades based on their strategies. This risk-free environment allows them to learn from both successful and unsuccessful trades, identify strengths and weaknesses in their approaches, and build confidence in their trading abilities.

The advantages of paper trading include risk-free learning, the ability to test multiple trading strategies, getting familiar with the trading platform, and eliminating emotional factors from the trading process. However, it's important to recognize that paper trading has its limitations, as it cannot fully replicate the psychological aspects of real trading, such as the emotional impact of gains and losses.

As traders gain confidence and experience in paper trading, they can gradually transition to trading with real money. When doing so, it's crucial to start with a small amount of capital, practice proper risk management, and continue to refine their strategies based on live market conditions.

Ultimately, paper trading serves as an essential steppingstone in a trader's journey, providing them with valuable insights and experience before they engage in live trading with real financial stakes.

www.ingramcontent.com/pod-product-compliance
Lightning Source LLC
Chambersburg PA
CBHW062359290526
45794CB00003B/1014